DEC 2016

# EARTH SCIENCE ROCKS!

# Minerals

by Chris Bowman

BELLWETHER MEDIA • MINNEAPOLIS, MN

Note to Librarians, Teachers, and Parents:

**Blastoff! Readers** are carefully developed by literacy experts and combine standards-based content with developmentally appropriate text.

**Level 1** provides the most support through repetition of high-frequency words, light text, predictable sentence patterns, and strong visual support.

**Level 2** offers early readers a bit more challenge through varied simple sentences, increased text load, and less repetition of high-frequency words.

**Level 3** advances early-fluent readers toward fluency through increased text and concept load, less reliance on visuals, longer sentences, and more literary language.

**Level 4** builds reading stamina by providing more text per page, increased use of punctuation, greater variation in sentence patterns, and increasingly challenging vocabulary.

**Level 5** encourages children to move from "learning to read" to "reading to learn" by providing even more text, varied writing styles, and less familiar topics.

Whichever book is right for your reader, Blastoff! Readers are the perfect books to build confidence and encourage a love of reading that will last a lifetime!

This edition first published in 2015 by Bellwether Media, Inc.

No part of this publication may be reproduced in whole or in part without written permission of the publisher. For information regarding permission, write to Bellwether Media, Inc., Attention: Permissions Department, 5357 Penn Avenue South, Minneapolis, MN 55419.

Library of Congress Cataloging-in-Publication Data

Bowman, Chris, 1990- author.
  Minerals / by Chris Bowman.
    pages cm. – (Blastoff! Readers. Earth Science Rocks!)
  Summary: "Developed by literacy experts for students in kindergarten through grade three, this book introduces minerals to young readers through leveled text and related photos"– Provided by publisher.
  Audience: Ages 5-8.
  Audience: K to grade 3.
  Includes bibliographical references and index.
  ISBN 978-1-60014-980-1 (hardcover : alk. paper)
  1. Minerals–Juvenile literature. 2. Mineralogy–Juvenile literature. I. Title.
QE365.2.B69 2014
549–dc23
                            2014002701

Printed in the United States of America, North Mankato, MN.

# Table of Contents

# What Are Minerals?

Minerals are the building blocks of rocks. Some minerals are made of one **element**.

# Earth's Layers

Earth is made up of the inner core, outer core, mantle, and crust. Minerals are found in the mantle and crust.

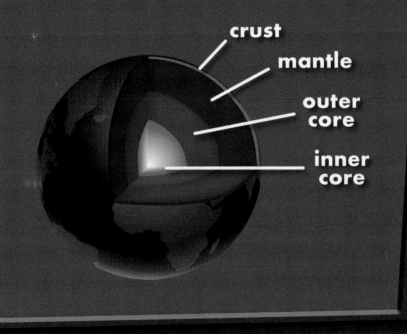

crust

mantle

outer core

inner core

Others are **compounds**. More than 4,000 minerals have been found so far!

Minerals are **inorganic**, natural **solids**. Each has its own properties. These include color, shine, and hardness.

# Mohs Scale of Hardness

The Mohs scale of hardness ranks minerals on their ability to be scratched. Diamond is the hardest mineral, and talc is the most easily scratched.

1 talc

6 feldspar

2 gypsum

7 quartz

3 calcite

8 topaz

4 fluorite

9 corundum

5 apatite

10 diamond

Mineral compounds form when elements in nature are brought together. This sometimes happens when **lava** hardens. It **crystallizes** into minerals when it cools.

Another way this happens is in water. Many elements are **dissolved** in the oceans and seas. As water **evaporates**, the elements join to become minerals.

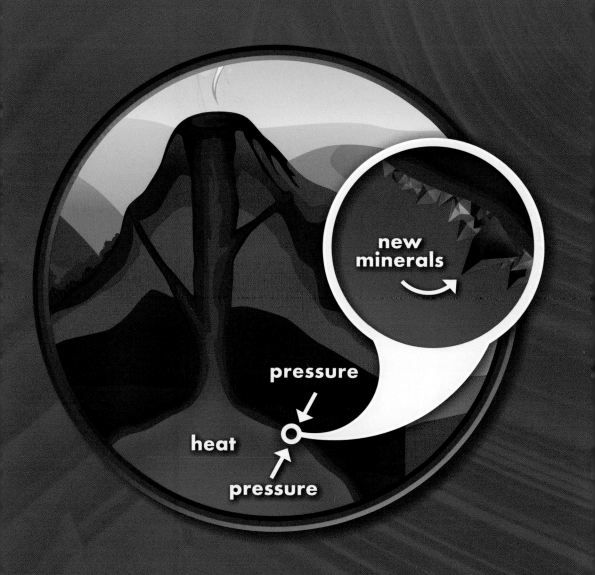

Other times minerals go through temperature and pressure changes underground. Then they **react** with nearby elements to make new minerals.

# Rock Cycle

igneous rock

magma
crystallization

weathering /
erosion

magma

sediment

metamorphic
rock

sedimentary
rock

# Types of Minerals

There are many kinds of minerals. They have different uses in daily life. Some minerals help people stay healthy. People need to eat foods that have iron and calcium.

**foods high in iron**

soy beans

spinach

steak

# foods high in calcium

yogurt

cheese

milk

The most valued minerals are called gemstones.

**diamond**

**ruby**

**emerald**

Some of these **rare** minerals are
diamonds, rubies, and emeralds.
They are often turned into jewels.

# Minerals as Clues

**Geologists** look at minerals to learn about the history of elements in an area.

This helps them figure out how
the land has changed over time.

# Searching for Minerals

Minerals are almost everywhere you look. Try to identify minerals in your backyard and by bodies of water. You will be an expert in no time!

# Be a Geologist!

## What you need:

**32-ounce mason jar**

**string**

**pencil**

**paper clip**

**2 cups of hot water**

**table salt**

1. Have an adult help you boil the water. Then pour it into the jar.

2. Pour salt into the water. Then stir to dissolve. Add enough salt so that it does not all dissolve.

3. Tie one end of the string to the pencil and the other end to the paper clip. Set the pencil on the top of the jar. Let the string hang in the water.

4. Let the string sit in the water for one day.

5. Check your string to see the crystals that have formed.

# Glossary

**compounds**—minerals that contain two or more elements

**crystallizes**—hardens to form crystals

**dissolved**—mixed into a liquid

**element**—a chemical substance that cannot be broken down further

**evaporates**—turns from a liquid into a vapor

**geologists**—scientists who study the earth

**inorganic**—not made by living organisms; inorganic materials are made by Earth's environments.

**lava**—hot, melted rock that comes out of volcanoes

**rare**—not occurring often

**react**—to change because of contact with another substance

**solids**—substances with stable shapes and volumes

# To Learn More

## AT THE LIBRARY

Hand, Carol. *Experiments with Rocks and Minerals*. New York, N.Y.: Children's Press, 2012.

*Rocks and Minerals: Facts at Your Fingertips*. New York, N.Y.: DK Pub., 2012.

Tomecek, Steve. *Everything Rocks and Minerals*. Washington, D.C.: National Geographic, 2010.

## ON THE WEB

Learning more about minerals is as easy as 1, 2, 3.

1. Go to www.factsurfer.com.

2. Enter "minerals" into the search box.

3. Click the "Surf" button and you will see a list of related web sites.

With factsurfer.com, finding more information is just a click away.

# Index